# Night Owling

## Poems

## Peter Roberts

'Night Owling'
© Peter Roberts

First Edition 2022

Published by Dempsey & Windle

15 Rosetrees
Guildford
Surrey
GU1 2HS
UK
01483 571164
dempseyandwindle.com

A catalogue record for this book is available from the British Library
British Library Cataloguing-in-Publication Data

ISBN: 978-1-913329-70-9

Printed and bound in the UK

For Bronwen – funny, smart daughter grown to wise woman who knows the pathways of love and the power of forgiveness.

## Acknowledgements:

Many people have encouraged and advised me in my poetry life and I'm grateful to them all, particularly:
- Marjorie Lotfi Gill and judges at Wigtown Poetry Prize
- Hugh McMillan and Stuart Paterson for their support
- Kenneth Steven's insightful and incisive mentoring
- Dumfries and Galloway Unlimited's financial support
- Chrys Salt, friend and tireless champion of my poetry
- Janice Dempsey at Dempsey and Windle for saying yes
- Annie Wright – most of all – for just about everything.


Some of these poems have been previously published:

*Kites at Auchenfedrick, Morecambe Bay 5th February 2004* and *Clougha* were published in Dreich Issue 10 (Hybrid Press, winter 2020).

*Along the Kali Gandaki 1982* was published in The Artist's Tale (Lit Room Press, 2019)

*Meadowsweet* was published in Summer Anywhere (Hybriddreich Ltd, 2021)

*Mary Timney's Rope* was published in No Stone Unturned (Crichton Writers, 2021)

*Night Owling* was published online by Wigtown Poetry Prize, and as a film poem at www.thebakehouse.info/bakings

*Beyond Criffel* was published online as a film by Wigtown Book Festival, and with *Curlew for Christopher* and *To The Far Side* at www.thebakehouse.info/bakings.

# Poems

# Night Owling
*after Alan Ginsberg and Edward Hopper*


...and wake sometime after one get up to take a leak come back to keep the beat with every toss and turn the night owl taunting with its high fluting hooting a bass/alto riff that goes on and on like Lester Young in Kansas in 1938 saxing the crowd to madness with 72 choruses of The Man I Love and worry about Moloch's latest incarnation creeping into my brain along wi-fi waves the clock going too slow to an ending too fast for hopes of sleep...

...and long to shout down the ghost howl of the insomniac and leave hunting like a nighthawk through dark frosted streets to that pool of light in the lonely night order coffee and corn dogs share the company of strangers in meaningless talk about the Bears and the Blackhawks anything so's to seem alive and not lost...

...and wonder why, last night, I dreamed of Chicago.

# Walls

The carriage is full, each passenger, like me,
hauling their life's baggage – the man drinking
whisky in the morning, boys gambling noisily,
the couple rigid with avoidance of each other,
me, as ever, travelling alone –
our stories like spells conjuring our paths.

We skirt the edge of debateable lands,
climb into two thousand years of history
heaving beneath a green skin,
poking, scratching, breaking through
to reveal only the skeletal remains
of old beliefs and their martial consequences.

And, stilled by motion, I feel again
the clawing of my own history
freighted in my chest, the iron weight
dragging at heart and lungs, the burden
of flesh built-up to wall the past,
incarcerate hurts that will not be silenced.

Where the track cuts the corner of a Roman fort,
like a release of trapped time, the train's struggle
eases and lets go into a freewheeling flight
towards the distant city, into the present.

## Nature Studies

Childhood was an orgy of killing:
blown larks' eggs, frogs imprisoned
in milk churn aquaria until they died,
eels that swam from the Sargasso
to the beck running down Pye's field,
only to be shot with bow and arrow.

Until my conscience was netted
inside a parabola drawn in cruel air
by a tumbling starling, felled
by my mindless catapult shot
into a flock gyrating overhead,
long before such murmurations

became a revered sight; before
a small somersaulting corpse
turned my mind, its arc of fall
a boundary set in empty space,
my first wall of awareness built
with burning shame, lasting guilt.

# Lost Northern Souls

*In every heart in every home / there's a dying man who lives alone.*

Jackie Leven, Classic Northern Diversions.

## Loonies

Run indoors: *there's a loonie coming, mam!*
And I'd stand at the bay window, watch him
shuffling up the lane, grey tweed coat and cap,
short steps up on his toes; the same quick time
all those men danced, a sure sign of madness
to a boy ignorant of their suffering.
It was the nineteen fifties, and parents
thought not to enlighten but to keep us safe.

I know now many of those broken men
were submariners, maddened by terror,
released from iron coffins to confinement
in our local looney bin, and feel shame
that we didn't know how to respect men
who gave their sanity to keep us safe.


## Outsider

Gadge was how we knew him; didn't know
it was Scots for a *man*, or traveller slang
for an *outsider,* but he filled those boots.
Came from who knows where to play football
for the Quernmore team, he used his body
like a hob-nailed missile, causing mayhem
in visiting sides, a good substitute
for actual skill and tactical nous.

He was hero and baddie to us young lads,
looked up to, kept at a distance, unknown.
We didn't care if he went home to family
or slept in a barn, never learned his name.
He was no more than Gadge, good for a laugh,
fouling, ballooning shots over the bar.

## Ambrose

Was he ever more than this silhouette,
driving the iron wheeled Fordson on patrol
along the far shore of Whittaker's field?
I knew only his seasonal presence,
the shit-stained gabardine, belted with string,
his anger when he caught us on the land.
Our childish mix of ridicule and fear
blinded us to the substance of the man.

I wonder if now there'd be a diagnosis,
some psychosis, from the war, maybe,
that shackled him to menial farm labour,
his disturbing, itinerant otherness.
But I'm grasping at shadows, wondering
how to see him. Perhaps on that tractor
he saw the sun setting fire to the bay
and we'd be joined, at the end of the day,

souls singing at the beauty of it.


## The Sheep Man

Dad took me with him once to see a man,
looked after the reservoir at Peddar Potts.
I can picture now a large balding head,
ruddy cheeks, a torn boilersuit, blood-stained
from slaughtering lambs in the barn, lived alone,
made tea as he and dad talked water work.
The only furnishing, a horse-hair couch, had spilt
its guts on the earth floor. I sat warily,

examined the room's strange decoration –
walls covered in show rosettes, mostly firsts,
prizes for his Rough Fells, he told me later,
talking with quiet passion of pin-width,
top-line, muscling; but taught me something else —
to see the man beyond appearances.

# Horizontal Hold

Dad...

Do you remember the first telly we had?
An entertaining but fractious child.

A passing truck, or jets flying overhead, testing
the sound barrier with impunity, would send it

into hysterics of flickering scanning lines,
a visual scream, and it was my job to reach

behind and twiddle the knob that settled
it down, brought it back into horizontal hold.

I didn't know then of the scenes off-screen,
especially after our uncle drowned and mam

went to pieces, without drama, still coping,
holding on, but all her spirit gone.

I see now that it was always you reaching
behind to make adjustments, keeping us held,

level, moving forward; making pictures
of futures for us all to walk into,

more vivid than any grainy, monochrome
nineteen fifties television show.

# Sapper Bateson's War

No end to the Battle of the Somme
for my granddad Benny Bateson.
Guns roared in the foxhole of his bed,
sixty years dying from his nightly dread.

My memories are of a Jekyll and Hyde.
As a lad I loved to be at his side,
tales of the old city always on his lips,
Grandstand on Saturday with pie and chips.

But he was Fuhrer in his own backyard.
He made my nanna's life grim and hard:
fireside chair, spittle sizzling on the grate,
'Another tea, Bel, and bring some bait'.

In time it was this face from which I turned,
and when I left home our bridges were burned.
I was a student and betraying his class
whilst he belonged to a time that had passed,

and his time had indeed stopped at the Somme,
shrapnel in his skull before the end of day one,
then a lifetime of waking, screaming in fear,
his private suffering year after year.

No counselling to help with the PTSD,
just *soldier-on sapper and keep your nose clean.*
No medals or dispatches to mark his valour,
He's not remembered on rolls of honour.

So I write these words to ask his forgiveness
for treating him with such cold indifference;
and to honour his name and his sacrifice,
for no peace came to him with the Armistice.

# Meadowsweet

In late summer, the dog-walking lanes
and overgrown flood meadows
brim with creamy flower foam.
At the Turning Tree or Big Bend Pool,
I may pluck a handful of the froth,
and rubbing, sniffing, scent another path,

back to that distant home of memory,
where you wait to wipe away tears
and bandage with wise words pride hurt
by the embarrassment of fall from bike or wall,
and releasing the same scent from its tin
apply your cooling salve to grazed knees:

the meadowsweet comfort of germolene.

## Autumn Skeins

The first geese arrived today
quilting the sky with ragged vees
from Svalbard to Solway

each skein an alliance
a honking team sharing the work
of unravelling distance

Hanks stretched between my hands
were wings flying to your lead
as you wound your skeins

your annual migration
knitting summer into winter
until your brood was flown

# Fading to grey

When did the fire start to fade from your hair?
Perhaps after you hid the boat I made
and told me you'd burned it? Or when I ran
to tell you that I'd caught twenty-three perch,
and you scolded me for telling lies. Maybe
it began long before, when you left me at
the gate of the children's home for staining
my new coat? But now I see the colour draining

from you when your brother, so much younger,
drowned, grief flowing with the blood from your wrists
at the sink, a washing-up accident
they said, but the stains spoiled everything.
Such grief that we began to ask, too late,
was it your brother who drowned, or your son?

# Manchester

## i. Crossing the Plains

It was a long journey, pre-motorway,
down from hill country to the grey flatlands
and drab red brick towns of South Lancashire.
*Watch out fer t'chip gobs*, my dad would say,
driving through Bolton, but I didn't get the joke —
dad's Mancunian snobbery about Bolton folk —
and was frightened, imagining letterbox mouths
into which I'd fall, my fear increasing at the sight
of ships' bows looming over the Salford dock wall.
Then we'd cross the rubble plains of slum clearance
a nothingness that disturbed me, alarmed
by spectral churches and pubs left standing
like the desert rock buttes in westerns.
And we'd arrive at *Nanna's-at-Manchester*


## ii. 6 Norman Grove

where there was no relief, my sense of dread
only deepened by dim, crumbling gothic.
Nanna, a tiny, dour, loud-mouthed harridan
from whom I cowered, lived in the back parlour,
hardly went out, seethed about *curry stink*
and *teddy boy louts*; other rooms abandoned
to trophies — ivory, masks, carved wood —
sent back by the grandad I never knew,
building railways in Africa, I understood.
Tea from Crown Derby with Chorley cakes,
then we'd escape into the building's dark heart,
retake the Alamo armed with elephant tusks,
stick hands in the maw of the leopard skin rug,
hide inside the mouldy elephant foot.

### *iii. Secret Friends*

Dad'd take the scores, *shh,* check his coupon,
pronounce Old Trafford's crowds to be clear,
and we'd leave, through the jungles of Ardwick
and Hulme, the ships' bows accentuating
my sense of doom. But every few miles,
they'd appear – man-in-the-moon faces,
stars shining in the night, my secret friends
lulling me back home to fields and hills.

Sixty years on, I remember, search the web,
find pub signs for Dutton's Brewery
of Blackburn, laughing boys raising a glass,
figures made from the letters O, B and J,
an acronym for the brewery's motto,
*Oh, Be Joyful*, meant just for me.

# Clougha

Clougha, hill of the cloughs, tumbled gritstone gullies
gouged by glacial water held, then breaking free,

two stave lines drawn across Birk Bank, where memory
reads the keynotes of our improvised ways to the top,

before access agreements, rules, paths, prohibitions,
before 'fell-walking' when this was just our child's play.

The name is a riff - *cloff,* percussive bass line
vibrating in the ravines, *ha* lifting, alto breeze

playing on summit rocks, tuned by the rising Lanky talk
of moors folk who first breathed out the word *cloffha*

like question, or challenge. The moor plays in the key
of *ha,* bleating of sheep, snipe drumming, curlew call,

*go-back-go-back* of grouse, heart thump as they launch
underfoot, the *hurr-haah* rasp of rotating querns,

the hand-turned millstones quarried here
since the first farmers, giving home its name:

Quernmore, a chaff of farms and barns scattered
beneath Clougha's deceptively mountainous face,

a pretension revealed only at the top, the hill no more
than the frayed hem of Bowland's ruched tablecloth.

Yet she gave me, eight years old, breathless at the trig point,
turning to wonder, *haah,* at the shock of space –

home, city, the bay, distant Lakeland fells –
the greatest gift: to see my place in the world,

and the places to go beyond it.

## Black Thorns

Seventeen; half-cut on Blackthorn Cider –
cut above the plebs drinking Woodpecker
on our scale of working-class snobberies –
we charged along blossom-white Lunesdale lanes
in Fluff's hot, souped-up moggy thousand van,
outwitting the cops — according to Fluff —
with a mazy route from The Highwayman
at Burrow-with-Burrow, home to scorned parents.

Blind to springtime's hedgerow confetti
blessing our raging route to the city,
on deeper into our separateness,
Fluff knew his way – the fledged engineer
flown to Detroit, chasing automotive dreams.
The rest of us drifting, our plans half-formed,

me half a lifetime to find what I wanted,
ways home to the blackthorn wilds' embrace.

# Along the Kali Gandaki, 1982

Deep, deep down runs Kali, four miles deep,
below the crystal mountains, time unwinding inexorably –
glacier melt, Nepal's soil, cremation ash –
into the infinite sea.

Against the flow rises a tide of commerce,
a sufficient economy scaled to a human back
or the heavy lifting of mule and dzho,
tump-lined and panniered, defying Kali's gravity.

And up-along go pilgrims, the sadhus and lamas,
all the castes of soul seekers, ascending from the flood plain
to the Place of Liberation beyond Kali's dark gorge –
Muktinath, where five elements mingle, source of all life.

Everywhere along the trail life teeters between rise and fall:
here a snot-nosed child bawling, the tide streaming round her.
Down there, in a deep well of shadow, a buffalo, placid
under a raised blade, an age-long moment of stillness, before

blade and head fall, and a stream of blood joins Kali's flow.
To face suffering and walk on – is it callousness, or something
new stirring, compassion maybe, acceptance of all that is,
all the faces of this joyous, generous place, its people

still living a tradition grown from our innermost being,
made manifest in mani stones, prayer wheels, stupas, flags,
a landscape of the soul's journey, rising against the flood,
falling back; and always, high above, deep within,

the crystal mountain, calling us forth.

# Easterly

For days the snow came in short flurries,
white on white, a Malevich meditation.

Now the land is bullied by bitter wind,
slopes blasted and scoured to frozen feld grau,

the colour of a Wehrmacht tunic,
under a gunmetal sky. Snow piling against dykes

exhibits the architecture of the land,
a Bauhaus sketch of scumbled white edged with black line.

In the sheltering lee of the house
the snow, undisturbed, is a minimalist ground

where birds display around the feeder,
a Kandinsky composition on white,

the only movement in a hushed land.
A quieting grown into an immense silence

smothers the media chatter
of forecasts, warnings, complaints

with the gift of winter stillness,
the land pared back to unadorned planes

of a bare modernism,
form dreaming of its coming fecundity.

# Islay Sketches

## 1. Dry Spell

He stopped by as we erected the tent
with some comment about not fancying it
in last night's wind; then, ignoring you,
told me he met his wife at *university;*
stayed on to *found* his own company;
found an old friend, now a *lieutenant colonel;*
had come to buy his year's supply of *malts;*
corrected the way I said Bruichladdich.

Dismayed by the status signalling that passes
for friendly overtures amongst men,
I tried to stay out of the game –
attuned to it, like him, but to a lower rung,
I'm done with knowing my place. I said
we must get on, to get out in the sun.

Today he grunted to my *hi,* didn't speak.
Later we heard him screaming at his wife –
her reversing directions had left their van
*four inches*! from their awning tent. I enjoyed
a moment of grim superiority –
still playing the status game, after all.

## 2. Shower

He emerged naked from the cubicle,
stood beside me as I hurried on clothes
over damp skin, showed a half-turned back
to him, casual-like, to hide ageing's
spread and shrivelling, glanced to take in
a goliath of a man whose face could pass
for that Irish actor, Belfast twang to match,
big black-and-silver-haired pecs, ripped abs and…

…no, don't go there, but he was the full man.
*Aye, it's a grand day,* he said. I mumbled
agreement, fumbled the door, and fled, disturbed
by nothing he did or said, more the ease
with which he carried himself, filled the space,
a lightness that cast me into the shade.

## 3. Storm

We returned from our trip to Sanaigmore,
reversed the van against the awning tent,
before spotting the first sign of trouble –
your shower cap halfway across the field,
and the front of the tent flapping, blown in.
Wind and rain had come from out of the blue
to mock our sun-rushed pegging and guying,
the groundsheet mapped with rivulets and pools.

No worries, you said, we'll soon get it mopped,
and I pretended the same demeanour.
But anger rose beneath the calm surface,
the need to deflect the shame of failure,
blame cracking the façade and breaking through,
a storm that came raging out of the blue.

## 4. Overcast, clearing later

I watched as you walked back towards the tent,
contemplating the cloud-pinked blue, smiling,
detached, miles away, when the thought hit me
like a punch, *I do not know you at all*,
and sensed walls of separation rising.
That night I lay listening to the tide
lapping into Loch Indaal, heard the breeze
rustle in the lung of the tent – reminded,

everything breathes to its own rhythms,
its seasons advancing and retreating.
We make ready for the stars to favour us,
fill us with the in-breath of connection,
and trust the ebb into separateness
will bring us again to new beginnings.

# Aesling

*for Jacob*


Born of Smith and Wright,
Anglo-Saxon trades, you are no Viking.
But grown from childhood in the shades of Aske
you may yet become Aesling, man of ash.

Warrior waiting to find your battles,
grasp your spear, aesc, Aske, hone its edges sharp
on these offered stones, to ready yourself
for what will surely come with time and trust.

Have courage – not absence of fear or despair,
but the strength to conquer them.

Remember Odin, who in sacrifice hung
from Yggdrasil, the world tree, the ash.
Raven took his eye, but he gained insight
and wisdom, letting go, to grow.

Be like the ash, strong, deep-rooted, resilient,
burn bright like firelight, embrace all of life –
the serpent and eagle, earth and the abodes of the Gods,
as if you are Yggdrasil.

Choose your battles as healer, protector, manifesting ash.
Just as you who grew in the shades of ash
are an Aesling, protected by ash spirit.

Believe it.

# Mary Timney's Rope

*after the stone rope carved by John Corrie in 1866*
*above the door of the Sheriff's Court in Dumfries*


Stop knots, like those tied in stone to the courthouse door,
would catch an uncleated sheet in the block; hold the clew
against the wind to keep a ship on course for home.

Or tell a stone parable about a town's course trimmed
to the winds of the law, though laws can be set wrong,
need a diligent watch keeping when they blow too strong.

There's a rigging stop knot called the single throat seizing.

I think of Mary Timney, half-mad with starvation
and fear for her weans, who in desperation
beat and murdered her neighbour, Ann Hannah.

She was strangled by the law on this very spot,
the last woman in Scotland to be publicly hanged,
the shame of Dumfries people, who wanted it stopped.

Three years later John Corrie carved a rope in stone,
in commemoration, they say, of our seafaring days,
but it's hard to believe his mind did not stray

to thoughts of Mary, swinging from her yardarm.
Perhaps he made her epitaph, and a proclamation
against such vile displays. Not that it worked

for Robert Smith; six years after Mary, the last man
to pay the law's due put on show to public view,
hanged on the same corner of Irish and Buccleuch.

# The Bowls Hut at Stroanfreggan


There are still places like this, where time reverses
off a slow road, unwinds from the turbines
on the hill, and whatever future lies beyond,
to listen: susurration of damp and mould
lifting felt from beds longing to be kissed again
by Taylor-Rolph, Drakes Pride, Henselite;
trapped echoes – clack of lignum vitae,
whispers between skip and hench of lambing,
the hay, prospects for the Dumfries tournament,
a shout of 'hog', their lead calling the head,

as their second kneels to the bed,
delivers his bowl through the rusting guard...

to where the tee in its house holds its breath,
yearning for the wood's slow, tender entry,
the score frame a clock stopped sometime around
nineteen ninety; the chairs waiting for them
to return from that night when they switched off
the light, closed the door, calling over shoulders,
'See ye next week', 'aye, see ye then',
only this time...they didn't.

And you, with your digital camera and time
to spare, contemplating the aesthetics of decay –
the pleasing contrast of rust-red roof, once-black walls,
the deep blue, empathetic snow on the Rhinns –
linger at the broken window for a glimpse
of a world unto itself, playing by its own rules,
receding into the distance on a slow road.

# Phenomenology

Lately in the woods at Auchenfedrick;
again today by Chanlockfoot: cryptic
cinnamon erupting from bracken, snap
of feather on air, the jouking dash through
old oak and hazel, long bill charting
a path from peripheral vision to gone...
no ornithologist, I read the clues
in field guides, hazard a guess at...woodcock?

A thing must be named to be fully seen.
Yet the naming mind is blind to such ringing
moments when the bright world enters aslant
the dark universe of the head, claiming it
for the instant before thought with movement,
colour, sound - the phenomenon of woodcock.

# History of Glencairn

This decaying land waits
for its true nativity,
when old men with no need of gain,
but who know no other way,

roam the glen in ancient jeeps,
dug in the back, orphan on the lap,
doing the rounds of scattered faulds,
rented or bartered, *tae keep ma haund in.*

Muir midwives, coaxing lambs from yowes,
new life birthed into rain, snow, rain again.
And each birth gathers the unravelling land,
calling it back to attention.

*I'm fair puggled*, they'll say, leaning on the yett,
*this yin's ma last year.* But they'll be back,
to keep the lambing and their own selves going
'til they and the land lie thegither.

# North by Newfoundland

Everything speaks of the north:
dark forests rolling to the mind's horizon,
shipwreck coasts battered by Atlantic storms,
icebergs drifting across summer bays,
humpback whales breaching silvered seas,
moose wandering on the Skerwink Trail.

Such memories, siren whispers, unsettle
these torpid hearth-bound days with thoughts
of Avalon, The Rock, that new-found land,
and stir my heart's desire to go, be young again,
unbridled, free, set my compass northwards,
cast my dreams way beyond the Hebrides.

Yet cast a dream back to the old world,
due east from Signal Hill or Heart's Desire,
and it will find its rainbow's end
not in some cold far northern place –
Iceland, Norway or even Shetland, say,
but in mid-France, Dijon, or Poitiers.

So, this dreaming north is not defined
by lines of latitude, but vagaries –
ocean currents, weather systems –
and by longing, desire's perception
that a land far to the south of here
is north beyond my imagination.

# Old White Man in Aberdeen

The conference at the Anatomy Rooms
was enthralled by his presentation
of a city transformed by a year of culture.

Yet when he disparaged *the old white men*,
though his meaning was clear, I felt
dismissed, excluded, put out to grass.

Outside, sunlight of Nordic clarity
made sparkling constellations of granite walls,
embraced people jostling along Union Street,

bounced pulses of connection from ships,
shining white and yellow at street ends,
to islands, rigs, and the vast north beyond.

The train carried us south, down home
along the scapula and spine of Scotland,
the old body politic reinvigorated.

The rails seemed to sing with an energy
that might build a new nation,
include us all, even the old white men,

who still carry within them a seed that,
if nurtured, may yet astound us.

# Morecambe Bay, 5<sup>th</sup> February 2004

*i.m. Mary Roberts*


This floating world, realm of earth
relinquished by land, dominion
of the moonstruck sea,

where evening's peach-pinks
and harebell blues fade to grey,
a curtain drawn on the dying day.

The tide slithers, creep-races unheeded,
slops into slacks, quickens sands, claims again
Yeoman's Wharf, Priest Skear, Mort Bank.

And you, a drowning linnet
relinquished by life, adrift on a distillation
of fear, memory, pretence,

feel the tug of the ebb-tide –

but this night's tide comes not for you.
Twenty-three migrant workers slaving
on Warton Sands to accrue

nine pence per pound of cockles –
adrift the moment they left Fujian –
have arrived at their final station.

From this distance it seems
your lives unfolded to common themes,
poverty, powerlessness, separation,

and even in the anguish of your dark night,
you find compassion for these strangers,
a final surge of the heart's tide.

# Curlew for Christopher

Your last email arrived with the curlews,
the day of spud planting – the spuds
and the curlews late, after the easterly blast.

And I wished your message later still or never.
*Only two or three months* you said, and I heard
a new acceptance in the way you phrased those words,

colder than the spuds' damp trenches.
And the cooor-lee call shivered down my spine,
wings folding like angels as they landed

in their water meadow nesting place,
spearing me with spectral sounds to the moors
of childhood, like spirits of springtime past,

whilst the postcards from your migrations
to Baltic summers and the world's lecture halls
were messengers from possible futures.

So, leaning into my digging I was held
in perfect balance between root and growth,
though I didn't know it or make the link

until I knew that you, and maybe one day
the curlew, will be no more.
My world will be diminished without you.

# Revolution, 30th January 1969
*after a photograph by Ethan A. Russell*


The camera seems to float above the city,
like some deity's eye, seeing this story
play out to its ending, waiting for the legend
to loosen from its rooftop scaffold
and ascend into mythology; join company
with the risen on their balustrade plinths
across the street — Leonardo, Titian, Raphael,

Wren, drawing rock sketches of a London
still recognisable, the skyline barely obtruded,
Portland stone, yellow brick smoked to grey,
hardly changed, perhaps like the lives of those
who say they want a revolution, listening below,
dark suited office boys, shop girls, porters
in uniform blue jackets, collar and tie,

the revolution playing out over their heads.

Even girlfriends and hangers-on huddled
by the chimney pots are washed out, colourless.
But Ringo's scarlet jacket is a struck match
fizzing sparks in four-four time across the roof,
carrying the music over the edge, down to the crowd,
the band's parting gift that, like them or not,
would be a yardstick for this generation

measuring everything that was to come.

# Kites at Auchenfedrick

*after 'Christ of St John of the Cross', Salvador Dali*


Red kites rattled by the in-bye gate, drop from ash
on the moor's edge, hook the liquid air and ascend
to float on pinioned wings
over this sodden northern Galilee.

First one, then two, and three,
each a heart's leap lifting, exult ascending,
until a circus of six circle the rim of land
under the tented sky.

I encircled, thought-staunched, eye entranced –
mastery of wing-plane dressing rough air,
deft tail swivel holding a line, lines weaving
a lucent roof over sanctified space.

Each cruciform grace lifts the darkling veil,
atoms of life unifying the universe –
pinions combing infinity, raptor eyes
fixated on the warrens of Auchenfedrick.

Louche brigands tumbling down the sky for joy
redeem my veiled heart, unkiltered spirit.

# To the Far Side

I tell myself this pond should be enough;
why struggle vainly for poetry from within?

It presents its small beauties and dramas
profusely to my writing room window,
my gaze hypnotised by the cadmium blaze
of whin bowing to its rippled twin, heavy
with its buttery coconut scent.

Here comes petty officer robin on patrol,
mounts the same perches on every watch,
puffs his red breast to assert his minor rank,
ignored by chaffinches fossicking the reeds
for soft furnishings for the second brood.

And, ah, the swallows, arriving on the dot,
swoop to dip and drink, climb, circle,
swoop again, like a frenzied dogfight
for a few minutes, and then are gone,
leaving a spirograph of ripples, fading.

But a crow, stalking the pond's bank —
its cocked black eye bright in its black nest,
spearing into the reeds to pull out a small frog,
stabbing, butchering, down in two gulps —
draws my eye beyond the pond to a submarine

sidling up the loch; and to the far side,
where below the sunlit mountain tops,
the forest is shadowed and mute, a cloak
silencing the land beneath, masking its shapes
and the broken remnants of lives lived on it.

Cold afternoon rain comes, stippling the water.
The birds are silent now. The rain stops,
and bubbles rise from the hidden world below.
This pond should be enough, but my heart insists
it's inwards to the silenced places I need to go.

## Beyond Criffel
*for Acky*

I'm on the other side of Criffel now.

At Glencaple's old tobacco quay,
the moonstruck river flows backwards,
a clock unwinding into memory.
The tide spools away from Criffel's reel,
upstream, threading this other country,

where we climbed Clougha as child's play,
became infected with longing
for the high fells across the bay.
Followed them north to Grasmoor,
from where Criffel, on a farther shore,

signalled where to go next.

I think of Liatach, running the scree,
our best, our final climb, the last day
it was all aligned, the hill,
you and me, our hill-made mind,
coming down fast in the sun's last rays.

A fragile freedom, giving way
to a life that led, fifty years on,
beyond Criffel to this riverside,
looking back to those hills of youth
across time's irreversible tide.

# Peter Roberts

Peter Roberts lives in southwest Scotland. He started writing poetry in 2016 and won the Fresh Voice Award at the Wigtown Poetry Competition in 2020. This is his first collection of poems. It is an insomniac's exploration of the emotional archaeology of family and early experience, the characters who peopled his childhood, a life shaped in its values and hopes by the hill country of the north. His poems also address ways of seeing, the evoking power of decaying human landscapes, loss and redemption, traits of masculinity… and, weaving in and out of the poems, birds, carrying the spiritual baggage with which we endow them.

Peter's poems have been published in print and online. He is an active participant in the vibrant poetry scene in southern Scotland and reads his work widely. He is part of the team that organises The Bakehouse poetry venue and Big Lit Festival in Gatehouse of Fleet. From 2015 to 2018 he led the project that won a Creative Place Award from Creative Scotland for his home community of Moniaive and Glencairn, and co-ordinated the three-year arts programme funded by the award. He is currently (2022) working on his next poetry project, Archipelago of Silences, exploring the making of masculinity.